Join my facebook coloring group and get a lot of free coloring books and coloring pages

IMPRESSUM / IMPRINT
Monsoon Publishing LLC
Email: info@monsoonpublishing.de
www.monsoonpublishing.de
facebook.com/monsoonpublishingllc

Monsoon Publishing LLC
www.monsoonpublishing.com
info@monsoonpublishing.com
facebook.com/monsoonpublishingusa

Printed in the USA
CPSIA information can be obtained
at www.ICGtesting.com
LVHW072332181223
766772LV00015B/681